The Story of Ci

To:
Autumn and Lucy
my greaties —
Ruth P. Crawford

by

Ruth Pangle Crawford

Catch the Spirit of Appalachia, Inc.
Western North Carolina

First Edition 2015

Layout /editing by Amy Ammons Garza

Publisher:
Catch the Spirit of Appalachia, Inc.—Imprint of:
Ammons Communications — SAN NO. 8 5 1 – 0 8 8 1
29 Regal Avenue • Sylva, North Carolina 28779
Phone/fax: (828) 631-4587

Library of Congress Control Number: 2015945183

ISBN No. 978-0-9965199-1-5

P R I N T E D   I N   T H E   U N I T E D   S T A T E S   O F   A M E R I C A

Dedication

I would like to dedicate this book to the wonderful train men who worked for Southern Railway on the Asheville to Murphy runs in the years 1928-1929. Their kindness meant the world to a little five-year old girl who was growing up in the mountains of western North Carolina.

Acknowledgements

In loving memory of my husband, Archie Crawford, who would be so proud of me for finally writing this book.

Jim Crawford and Karen Nicholson, my children, who have heard this story many times as they were growing up, but didn't really appreciate the true meaning of it until much later.

Kristi Nicholson and Julie Albert, my granddaughters, and my great-grandchildren: Kristopher Nicholson, Elizabeth Albert, Kenny Albert, and Jamie Albert.

Introduction

*L*ooking back, I now realize I was raised a child of the earth. Isolated on a mountainside, my father, mother, brother and I lived along the railroad tracks near Barker's Creek, North Carolina. Our home was a very modest house, with the fireplace providing the only heat. With heavy snow in the wintertime, our house was usually cold. We had no indoor plumbing, but we did have electric lights.

With all the work our family had to do to survive, I was never spared. I was always expected to do my share. My brother, JC was two years older than me, but I worked as hard as he.

I loved to hear stories told by my parents. Sometimes my mother would fix popcorn, and we would all sit around the fire and listen to Dad tell stories about World War I. He didn't like to talk about it, but if we begged him, sometimes he would.

I especially loved my mother's story about the day she got married. She had made a beautiful white dress for the wedding, and they secretly slipped off to the railroad tunnel which was near her parent's house in Barker's Creek. They had just begun the ceremony when they heard a train whistle. She had to back up against the tunnel wall as the train came through and was not happy that her dress got dirty.

After the train went through, they were able to

finish their "I do's."

When my father got out of the army, jobs were scarce. He worked for a while with a friend, Willis Sutton, in a hardware store in Dillsboro. Then they found jobs as loggers.

My brother, JC, and I were not as close as I would have liked. He was a typical boy.

We had big snows and my brother and I would take our sled and go up the mountain where we would have a long ride. There was a barbed wire fence at the bottom and we had to hold the wire up for each other as we came down on the sled. Sometimes my brother would drop the wire just as I was going under. Ouch!

There was no road to my house. Our house was about two miles up the railroad from the Revis Country Store located near the bridge by the highway. The only way to get there was to walk the railroad tracks. There had been an old logging trail at one time, but we never used it.

By the time I reached five years old, I loved to watch the train as it would come around the bend with steam billowing from it's smoke stack.

Three times a day, a train would pass by. . . I knew exactly what time it would come. The trains, their conductors and the people who rode would wave at me, and, standing on a rock, I would wave back!

These friendly people became welcome visitors to my lonesome world. I began to feel as if they were my family. This ritual became the highlight of my day.

And this is where Cinder's story begins. . . .

The Story of Cinder

In the distance, I heard the train whistle. I knew it would soon be coming around the bend. I flew off of the porch, running as fast as I could to get to my rock just above the railroad tracks. My heart beat fast as I saw the steam puffing above the tree-tops. There it was! And there was the conductor waving at me. I jumped up and down and waved back. The others on the train were smiling and waving also. I waved until the train was out of sight.

The train was gone. Slowly, I climbed down off of the rock and walked back up the trail.

Christmas would soon be here. Each year my mother would tell my brother and me the Christmas Story. She had also told us all about how Santa Claus would bring us toys and me a baby doll. This had never happened. We would only get oranges and maybe a few sticks of candy.

Our Christmas tree was usually a small one where we made our own decorations out of paper and popcorn chains.

As I walked, thinking about the coming holiday, I wished, as always, for a doll of my own. In my heart I knew it couldn't happen, but I wanted one so much.

The next day, the weather grew colder, with snow everywhere. I had heard Daddy talking about 1928 being the coldest he had ever seen. Then, there was the train whistle! I ran to wave at the men on the train.

Something was strange.

I couldn't understand why the train was coming so slowly. I thought it was going to stop. When it got closer I could see men standing at the steps and the engineer was looking out his window. Another man was standing on the steps of the caboose.

When the train was in front of me, I could see one of the men had a large box in his hands and a big smile on his face. He stooped down and gently threw it over in the grass in front of me. He motioned toward it and at me.

As the train left out of sight, I ran over with my heart pounding, and picked up the big brown box. It was so big, and just a little heavy for me. A red ribbon was on top.

Oh, I thought...what could it be? For a moment I stared down the now empty railroad track.

Then, I ran home as fast as I could and asked my mother if I could open it.

As my mother watched, I carefully opened the box. Inside was the most beautiful doll that you could imagine. She had on a long, white dress. She had long, black hair. She could open and close her eyes. She could cry.

I had never been so happy. I named my doll Cinder to remind me of the train.

The next day I took Cinder with me when I ran to wave.

16

Everybody on the train was watching for me, smiling big smiles. We all waved and waved until the train was out of sight.

After I grew older, I realized those men must have had a very Merry Christmas, too, for they surely had known they had made a little girl very, very happy.

As time went on, Cinder became a part of everything I did, especially since I was alone most of the time.

JC talked about school and what they did there. I became excited about going also. . .for I was six years old now, and I knew I could go to school with him.

And then, Mother became very ill, confined to her bed in the back room.

One day my daddy came to me and said he couldn't find anyone to stay with Mother, or to take care of the cooking and cleaning the house.

He said it would have to be me.

"But, Daddy," I said. "I'm only six, and I don't know how to cook."

"You'll learn," he told me.

I began to cry. I was not going to be able to go to school and meet new friends.

So, I had to do all of the housework. My mother would call out cooking directions to me from her bed and I would try to make meals like she used to make.

The first time I made biscuits, Mother told me to get the bowl down and put in some flour. Then I was to

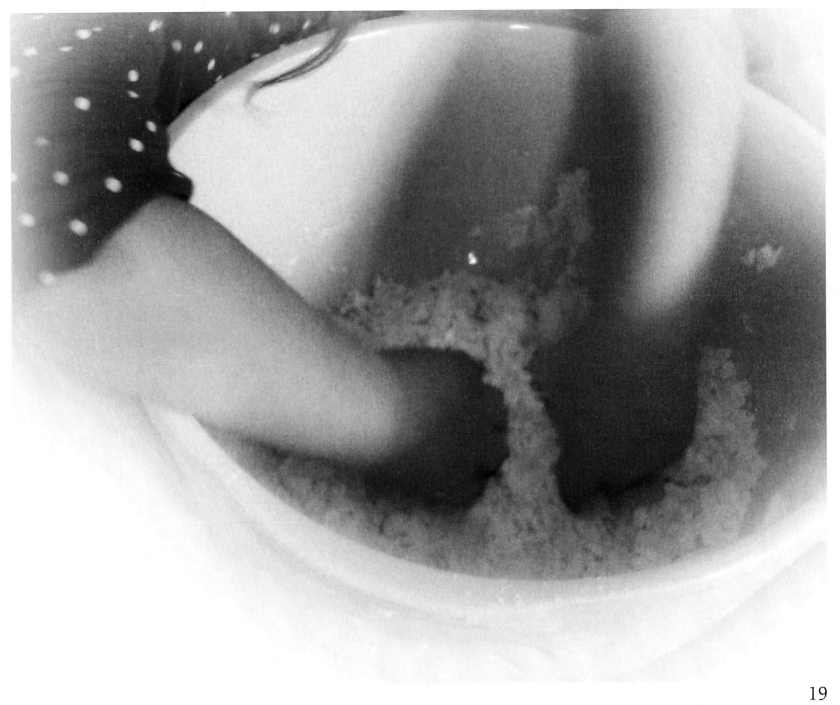

19

make a hole in the middle of the flour.

I made a little hole with my finger. She told me to swish it around to have a bigger hole, big enough to add the lard and milk.

When the biscuits came out of the oven they were so hard my brother wouldn't eat his and threw it out on the porch. One of our dogs, Fred, came over and sniffed the biscuit and he wouldn't eat it either!

Daddy did eat the biscuits, though.

Each day, I told my troubles to Cinder. She understood and sympathized with me. I don't know what I would have done without my Cinder.

Mother did finally regain her health, and I was able to go to school. Since the grades were all in the same room, I was able to catch up and even pass others who were my age. Cinder really loved that!

I loved walking to school, for I would pass the beautiful flowers along the way. My most favorite of all flowers was Queen Anne's Lace.

Years passed where other family tragedies affected my life. Through all the calamities, Cinder still listened. When I would cry, she would cry; when I would hide, trembling with fear, she would fill my arms and heart with her love.

When I was fifteen years old my family moved to the state of Washington, where I graduated from Hoquiam High School in Hoquiam, Washington in 1940. My father once more found work in the logging industry. Although I really wanted to take Cinder with me, my mother had told me to pack all of my belongings for storage

in one room of our house at Barkers Creek.

I had carefully put Cinder in a box and put her in the storage room. We had ridden to Washington on a train, and that made me miss my doll even more.

When we returned to Jackson County two years later, I was heartbroken to find that my precious doll, Cinder, was missing. In that moment, it seemed as if someone had stolen the best treasure I had ever had of my childhood.

******

In 1943 I married Archie Crawford. Soon afterward, he left to serve in World War II. When he returned unharmed, it was one of the happiest days of my life.

One day I told him about Cinder, the train, and my Christmas story. He said we should give a doll to a little girl every Christmas.

So, in the years afterward, we gave little "Cinders" to small girls every Christmas. But I don't believe there has ever been the magic there was on that lonely December day almost 87 years ago when the little girl with the long black hair ran down the hill and found Santa Claus on the train.

Still, it has warmed my heart to know that Cinder is continually bringing joy at Christmastime.

In 1975 I opened a gift shop in Dillsboro called The Country Shop. It was a perfect location for me – right beside the railroad tracks! I also had a wonderful stock of beautiful dolls!

Every time I heard the train coming, I would go outside and wave at the engineer.

To this day, I still love trains and those train men who wave and spread happiness throughout the land.

******

Epilogue

Throughout the years my husband, Archie, supported me in my endeavors to remember Cinder and the importance of what others might call just a simple doll.

Because of who he was and what he had gone through in his life, he knew little things meant a lot. It broke my heart to lose him in the late 1990s.

My children, grandchildren, and great grandchildren have heard the story of Cinder all of their lives.

Front row left to right: Kenny Nicholson, son-in-law; Jamie Albert, great granddaughter; Karen Crawford Nicholson, daughter
Back row left to right: Kenny Albert, great grandson; Elizabeth Albert, great granddaugher; Julie Nicholson Albert, granddaughter;
Kristi Nicholson, granddaughter; Kristopher Nicholson, great grandson

Jim Crawford (son) and Chip

My friends have also heard the story. So, one day in the summer of 2006, I was not really surprised when two good friends, Joe Rhinehart and Elizabeth Ann Stonesifer (EA), said they were coming by to pick me up for a trip. They wanted to drive up to Barkers Creek to see the old house and the rock where I stood to wave at the train.

There is now a road up to our old house and we could have driven all the way in, but Joe wanted to stop before we got there, and walk the distance to the railroad track and my "rock."

The next thing I knew, they brought out a box with a ribbon around it. I couldn't believe my eyes when I opened it and saw a doll exactly like my beloved Cinder.

Joe Rhinehart

Elizabeth Ann Stonesifer (EA)

It really touched my heart that these two friends knew how much the doll meant to me. They told me they had been searching for a long time to find the "perfect" replacement.

Her clothes had been made to look just like Cinder's from an old photo. EA, as an antique dealer, had found the doll, and even had ordered her hair from France.

I was just speechless.

Cinder had come home!